Consolations in Exile

Jean Bodin

Consolations in Exile

Off Duty – Man Versus the Volcano
The Nurse
Half the Sky: Missing Homer's Tough City

Jean Bodin

edition lulu/2013

1 Off Duty – Man Versus the Volcano

Episodes

Chorus, Giri, Givola, Michelle

Chicago, behind closed doors, today.

"When it is evening you say, 'It will be fair weather, for the sky is red'; and in the morning , 'It will be foul weather today, for the sky is red and threatening.' Hypocrites! You know how to discern the face of the sky, but you cannot discern the signs of the times." (Matthew 16:2-3)

1. Review Offers Some Hope

Chorus:
> The only sounds were wind and wheezing as we pressed
> on into the cradle of the sky.

Giri:

He said he hoped the once the dust settled on the sequester, the two sides could pivot to renewed discussion of tax and entitlement overhauls. "It may take a couple weeks," he said. "It may take a couple of months."

Chorus:

"Led by a cloud by day and a pillar of fire by night". Finally, we reached the top and peered into the volcano's caldera. Steep, jagged rocks guarded darkness.

Givola:

My "baby" is a Labradoodle called Dutch. We wanted to call her Coco but too many people have dogs called Coco. She has a very good appetite and loves it when I bring home leftover bison from the Four Seasons. I sauté it with green vegetables and serve it with a little bit of Fromm Surf and Turf [grain-free dog food] and a dash of Primadophilus [probiotic]. She loves it!

Chorus:

"They had to make some very, very hard decisions, and

none of the solutions are good, but you just have to make the best of what you have," he said.

Michelle:

The police watchdog said that it opened an investigation into the death of the man. The Independent Police Investigative Directorate said a postmortem showed the cause of death to be head injuries and internal bleeding. It noted other unspecified injuries. The speaker said a second postmortem will be presented but declined to give further details.

Chorus:

Roped together, Givola and Giri moved forward. Ten paces, break, repeat. The surface of the glacier was slick, but crusted with the residue of old snowfall. "Slam every step into the frozen stuff," Givola said. Giri made sure not to tread lightly. It felt good to be on a rock-free surface, even as it veered upward at a 40- and then 50-degree angle.

Giri:

I go out and pick mushrooms. I don't think it's very legal – they're on someone else's property, and they probably don't want me to pick them – but they're hen-of-the-woods, the best. We sauté them or roast them. Sometimes I pick so many I have to bring them to the food bank.

Michelle:
The video couldn't be independently verified, but police and the watchdog haven't denied the accuracy of what was recorded in daylight before a crowd of people.

2. Overhaul that hasn't had much success yet

Givola:
You have to serve excellent Champagne. I wouldn't go with Prosecco, but I'd serve a Franciacorta from Ca'del Bosco or Cavalleri, or a really beautiful pink Champagne, like Dom Pèrignon. Moët & Chandon Ros'e is another superb bottle.

Giri:

> Givola and I are close, but we don't generally tie our-
> selves together. He does things I wouldn't – like pick a
> tattoo off a parlor wall (hummingbird). I had never let
> my brother guide me up a slick ice sheet before, but
> I had no alternative; I didn't possess the skills to go it
> alone.

Givola:

> We really like to entertain outside. We have a very
> large deck that we built ourselves, and I love to barbe-
> cue on my Lynx professional grill. Last Easter, I grilled
> incredible ham.

Chorus:

> We'd be satisfied if he'd be satisfied flesh-bound when
> found for his bones risen. We live in freedom by ne-
> cessity, as the poet says, a mountain people dwelling
> among mountains.

Michelle:

> A spokesman for the police didn't respond to requests
> to comment.

3. Stern Action Should be Taken

Givola:

>We have seven beehives in our backyard and make honey every year. We also have a shower outside, and the bees come and check on me there. Even though it's difficult, making honey is definitely worth it; I love being able to make something that's 100% pure.

Giri:

>The rope theoretically increased our chances of survival: If one man slipped, the other could arrest his fall with a wing of the ice axe. Nonetheless, as we slowly inched forward, I questioned the logic of this setup. I tried to focus only on my footing.

Michele:

>"Yes there are challenges and we shall deal with them," the Commissioner said. "What is in the video is not how the police....goes about its work." Love gave the power, but took the will, they say. What if it wasn't all it should be?

Chorus:

Headphones that wrap around the back of your head may seem old-school, but when you put on these, you realize there's a lot to love about the classic form. The band seems to float behind your head – only a slight pressure tells you that it's there at all. Since the buds don't go too deeply into your ear canals, you get a good dose of outside noise – not enough to interfere with sound quality, but plenty to hear an oncoming bus.

4. Charged in Dragging Death

Givola:

We needed to make it another half mile, tied to the same short cord. Then we'd be on top.

Giri:

I briefly lost my nerve, however, when I saw butterflies entombed in the ice. And then a plane flying at eye level, a curious sight to behold. "That was a plane, right?", I asked Givola. "Yes," he replied. "And that's a baby crevasse," he added, smiling sheepishly. Fortunately, the long crack in the ice ahead of us was only an inch wide.

Chorus:

When you're entertaining at home, if you have incredible guests, you don't have to worry about anything else. Candlelight is beautiful, and we use old Venetian glasses – the short ones without the stems. They're much more fun.

Giri:

"We'll be fine," Givola said, stepping over the tiny fissure in the glacier's surface.

Michelle:

"It's obvious that his rights were violated in the most extreme way." "The behavior of the suspended members is condemned. . . in the strongest terms." But this story was different. It was raw, immense, and too close to home.

Chorus:

"When you are not wanted in, you want in, but maybe making you want in is the sense of a door, its purpose."

5. Why not Four Terms, and What About Michelle?

Givola:

I have so many cookbooks. I like "A Platter of Figs and Other Recipes." But I love the cookbook of my favorite dishes that my wife compiles. It's spectacular. Some day we should publish it.

Giri:

At 18,000 feet, the atmospheric pressure was half what you experience standing at sea level.

Chorus:

"There's so much to see," Givola said. He was talking about the landscape spread out below us, of course. But also the world.

Michelle:

The video showed four police officers strapping the man's wrists to a bench inside a police van. Two police officers then stood behind the van holding his feet as the vehicle started to move, before dropping the man's feet on the ground and allowing him to be dragged along the pavement. "We need you to sign off on everything," he replied in a joking tone.

Michelle:
    Givola is pioneering a whole new form of masculinity.

Chorus:
    He is a creep, a good looking creep, one of those whose eyes seem like spy holes for the demiurge of creepiness to peep on creation. He is all over the teleprompter.

Giri:
    Find semblance of rhythm in the strikes.

Givola:
    Don't pause too long or you'll lose your sense of the task.

Giri:
    What the hell is that? At rust in rotting shed?

Givola:
    Then come boils, and numbness, and blindness.

Giri:

> And the casualties keep coming, leaking and moaning.

Michelle:

> As if on a baggage carousel of disaster.

Givola:

> Go on, old boy. Pound away. Get that nail in there.

Giri:

> Get to work. Find some semblance of rhythm in the strikes.

Chorus:

> Life sucks, bad things happen to good people, all of that, but Michelle turns away quite leisurely from the disaster. Moving naked over Acheron, victor and conquered together. "Hear without listening. Breathe without asking." Behind closed doors reflect: the place was not worth stopping for...

(End)

2 The Nurse

Monologue to a web cam

Aphrodite's Fontana Amorosa, Pafos

The character's ring finger is longer than the index finger. Research shows that testosterone can be measured by the ratio between the two; her fingers suggest she has as much testosterone as a man.

I. My You

Forgive me
wake up and close the eyes
be kissed.
I am too
be not quite sure
how to respond
but nice of us even

(Look! Look! Wenches! You get the face you earn.) I was just 21 when I went to work for him. Like the other young women he hired as nurses, I had grown up in Ukraine. I didn't speak a word of Arabic, didn't even know the difference between Lebanon and Libya, Hamas or Hashemite. But "Papik," as we nicknamed him — it means "little father" in Russian — was always more than generous to us. (It feels good to me to be nice. It is a return-on-investment deal. I get so much more out of the day when I'm nice to people. You get paid off in spades that way, it's incredible.) I had everything I could dream of: a furnished two-bedroom apartment, a driver who appeared whenever I called. But my apartment was bugged, and my personal life was watched easily.

For the first three months I wasn't allowed to go to the palace. I think Papik was afraid that his wife, Safia, would get jealous. (It was math, it wasn't personal. Some people make all this stuff personal and it's not.) But soon I began to attend to him regularly. The job of the nurses was to see that our employer stayed in great shape-in fact, he had the heart rate and blood pressure of a much younger man. We insisted that he wear gloves on visits to Chad and Mali protect him against tropical diseases. That's no more his hand than it's Jesus Christ's, we said. We made sure he took his daily walks around paths of his residence, got his vaccinations, and had his blood pressure checked on time.

I do not regret what I do feel and say and do demand sleep with my kisses on your lips.

The foreign press called us Gaddafi's harem. That's non-sense. (It's nasty. If someone does that to me, I have the ability to never knowing their name again, I don't care about them , and they're still walking around in their shoes.) None of us nurses was ever his lover; the only time we ever touched him was to take his blood pressure. (Were they jealous? I don't know. Jealousy's not even on the radar screen for me. But it really hurt my feelings and

I decided to throw everything in – as girly as it sounds...)
The truth is that Papik was more discreet than his friend,
the womanizer Silvio Berlusconi. Gaddafi chose to hire
only attractive Ukrainian women, most probably for our
looks. He just liked to be surrounded by beautiful things
and people. He had first picked me from a line of candi-
dates after shaking my hand and looking me in the eye.
(I'm known for the call, but I'm not a one-hit wonder at all.
I was loaded for bear that entire time. Meaning I didn't
miss a beat the entire crisis, and so it wasn't one call, it
was all the calls.) Later I learned he made all his decisions
about people at the first handshake. He is a great psy-
chologist. (I am grateful that I've got name recognition –
not since then has there been anyone with name recogni-
tion.) And while observing and documenting these data
points, I will also witness the more elusive mysteries of
eel migration. I am amazed anew at the paradox that
our sense of place is derived from everything we know –
along with everything that causes us to wonder.

II. Sleep Well

Sleep well
no intimate and harrowing

passages fired
by fierce desire

with varying degrees of hope
nuanced and persuasive.

Papik had some odd habits. He liked to listen to Arab music on an old cassette player, and he would change his clothes several times a day. He was so obsessive about his outfits that he reminded me of a rock star from the 1980s. Sometimes when his guests were already waiting for him, he would go back to his room and change his clothes again, perhaps into his favorite white suit. When we drove around poor African countries he would fling money and candy out the window of his armored limousine to children who ran after our motorcade; he didn't want them close for fear of catching diseases from them. He never slept in a tent, though! That's just a myth. He only used the tent for official meetings. It was his stage, where he won his many battles for his cause – "with perceptiveness and conviction born of a lifetime of crusading" as my driver liked to say. (What happen to that driver? Was he a hidden jihadist? Justice through injustice? Freedom for what?)

So much for that.

We traveled in great style. I accompanied Papik to the United States, Italy, Portugal, and Venezuela, and whenever he was in a good mood, he asked us if we had everything we needed. We would get bonuses to go shopping. And every year Papik gave all his staff gold watches with his picture on them. Just showing that watch in Libya would open any door, solve any problem we had. When revolution came, I realized the cost.

From all my heart I wish you rest reflection spirit.

I got the impression that at least half the population of Libya disliked Papik. The local medical staff was jealous of us because we made three times more than they did- over $3000 a month. It was obvious that Papik made all the decisions in his country. He is like Stalin; he has all the power and all the luxury, all for himself. When I first saw television pictures of the Egyptian revolution I thought, nobody would dare to rise against our Papik. But there was a chain reaction after Tunisia and Egypt. If Papik had passed his throne to his son Saif when he still had the chance, I believe that everything would have been all right. People would not be in such a mess right now. Though completely translucent, glass eels reveal little about themselves. If you look closely, you can see their tiny eyeballs and hearts. But counting them is like trying to count something that is nearly invisible.

III. Too Demanding

Yes, I am but me.

I got out of Tripoli at the beginning of February, just in time. Two of my friends stayed behind, I never heard from them again. Foreigners were killed first. I had a very personal reason for wanting to get out: I was four months pregnant, and I was beginning to show. I feared that Papik would not approve of my Serbian boyfriend. I checked

the dictator's heart and lived in luxury. Considering this small fish with such giant inscrutability, I wonder if for all the reasons there are to count eels – or bald eagles or jellyfish or monarch butterflies – it is this convergence of the known and the unknown that most engages the human imagination. Back then I thought, Papik will probably never forgive me my betrayal. But I realized I did the right thing to flee Libya. My friends all told me I should think of my future baby and run. And I did.
The rest is not my history. The civil war and the NATO-led-military intervention resulted in the ousting and death (or should I say murder?) of him, and the collapse of his 42-year "First September Revolution" and 34-year-old Jamahiriya state. Videos of his last moments show rebel fighters beating him to death. There is also the rumor, that a French agent between them secured his killing. His body was publicly displayed in a freezer in Misrate until the afternoon of 24 October. Some people, I have read, drove hundreds of kilometres across the country to see proof that he had died. (How many of them have licked his boots just a year earlier?) A Dubai based satellite TV channel Al Aan TV showed amateur footage of the funeral in an undisclosed location in the desert next morning.

Weary she lies upon her cushions, where
once his chains crept over the bed and
held it fast, learning its guilty secret.
And so he, on attaining his desire,
as a reward put the eagle in the sky.

I escaped in time. He chose his destiny for himself. Last but not least, as I heard often in thousand and one days "God made the pharaoh as an example to the others". For me, that's reason enough to look to the eels this spring. Reason enough to check the net, to count the eels and weight them. Reason enough to note cloud cover, precipitation, the temperature of the air and water, the clarity and conditions of the tide. (What is true, I say, is that you get the face you pay for.)

(End)

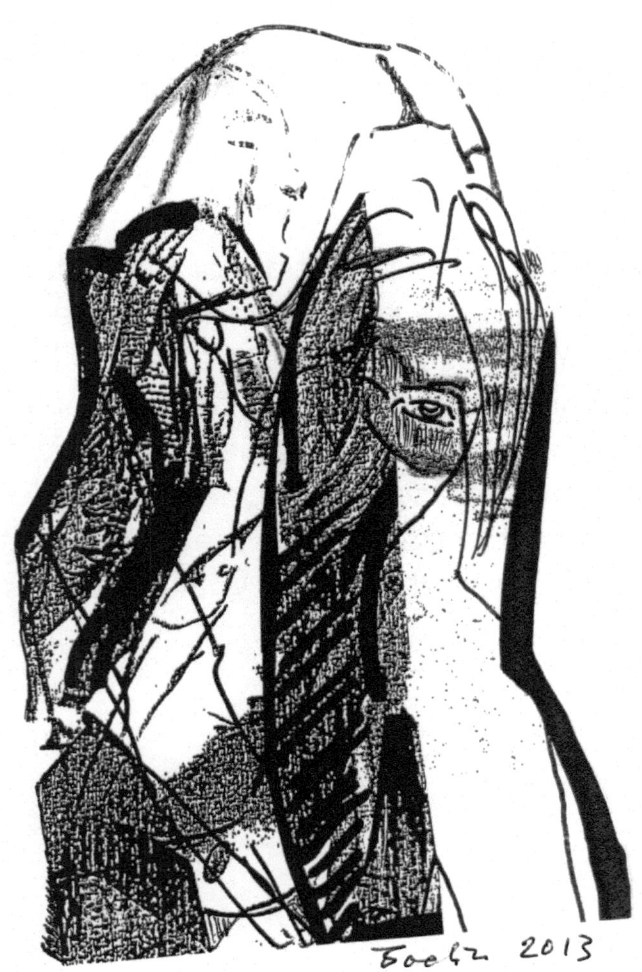
Боб? 2013

3 Half the Sky: Missing Homer's Tough City

Fact-based tale
recalling the cry of William Blake:

> *O Rose thou art sick.*
> *The invisible worm...*
> *Has found out thy bed*
> *Of crimson joy;*
> *And his dark secret love*
> *Does thy life destroy.*

Chorus of three –

Lucky Guy

Big-Speech-Sentimental

Swaggering Reporter

Spring in Delaware

1 ...conflict of interest

Chorus:

Is a businessman different from a military officer? If the president is a general, should his son not be a general? I speak to those who know; to those who don't my mind's a blank. I never say a word.

LG:

"You know, as humans, we can identify galaxies light years away, we can study particles smaller than an atom, but we still haven't unlocked the mystery of the three pounds of matter that sits between our ears," Mr. Obama said.

BSS:

Mr. Abe said that the central bank's "first goal" was to "display a strong commitment to create so-called inflationary expectations", which would ultimately lead to the 2 per cent target's being reached.

SR:

"Mr. Bakrie has nine lives - and he's only used six to date."

BSS:

We are the old, dishonoured ones, the broken husks of men.

Chorus:

Welcome home from the wars, Lucky Guy, long live your joy.

BSS:

Look for the smoke – it is the city of your devil laugh even now, a skeleton of color. The storms of ruin live!

LG:

Now the darkness comes to the fore, now the hope glows through your victims, beating back this raw, relentless anguish gnawing at the heart. There are very complex and difficult questions of law that I can see out there on the horizon. Each Troy is always liable to fall.

Chorus:

There's an ancient saying, old as man himself: men's prosperity never will die childless, once full-grown it breeds.

SR:

    The hoard was preheroic. The storm comes again, the crashing chords! In the event of a shooting, he said, "the presence of armed security personnel adds a layer of security and diminishes response time." When they tell you it's only a myth don't believe them.

2 …his attitude to business

Chorus:

    Everything is for sale at the right price. You should not fall in love with a company. You should only fall in love with your wife. Most of those cases will settle discreetly, with no trace of evidence in court files or Finra records.

SR:

    They spare nothing, eager to build its heat, "the economy is a living thing and we don't know what will happen around the world. What is important is to aim steadily for the target." Gods of the earth and public markets – all the altars blazing with your gifts!

LG:

Even then I told my people all the grief to come.

SR:

Not by rank but chance, "reach a level of research and development not seen since the height of the Space Race". Oh for a blessed end to all our pain, some godsend burning through the dark –

BSS:

There. Have I hit the mark or not? Invisible worm. The pain of pain remembered comes again. A terrible gift is a gift in a terrible world. This is a show that, after all, privileges talk of maggots in the scrotum, against which matters of feeling and empathy might be hard-pressed to compete.

Chorus:

Cry, cry for death, but good win out in glory in the end.

3 ...his biggest weakness

Chorus:

I am too kind-hearted. I'm too generous towards people who fail...people who betray us...towards our enemies. Memory womb of Fury child-avenging Fury!

LG:

Conquer with compassion. Then the gods shine down upon you, gently. "We have engaged fully with the data protection authorities involved throughout this process, and we will continue to do so going forward," it said in a statement.

Chorus:

Tell us the news! What you can, what is right. Heal us, soothe our fears!

LG:

No, what do you mean? I can't believe it. "People in the mudflow – 99 per cent of them – are thankful to me and to the family...because they got more than they had before," he says. If I can live by what I say, I have no fear.

BSS:

True, we have done well. He would divert most of the funds into providing free public education and much-needed health programmes. He also pledges to be "much firmer" in defending religious diversity. The tears fill my eyes, for joy.

LG:

Positioning himself to take a less aggressive, more reasonable position, late but true to revenge, a stabbing Fury!

SR:

Oh, crimson joy, which provides intuitive updates based on calendar entries, location patterns and emails, is one example of a service making use of the new approach. And who on earth could run the news so fast?

Chorus:

A Broadway hit that's not a musical. Ill-equipped to handle the painful truth. Would it be bad form to wear this hat? Will the ice creams cause indigestion? The narrow plot I love the best. And now I salute the land.

(Music: "When the Saints Go Marching In")

(End)

Notes

Off Duty – Man Versus The Vulcano written spring 2012; public reading at 13th ISSEI International Conference, University of Cyprus, July 2-6, 2012; electronically published in the conference proceedings at `http://hdl.handle.net/10797/6255`

The Nurse written spring 2013, first version

Half The Sky: Missing Homer's Tough City written winter 2013, first version

Comments

Off Duty's episodes spin audacious, even deviant fables about contemporary American politics and culture. But rather than projecting familiar characters in logical events, Bodin seems to be intent on inspecting the fragments of broken lives, de-constructing situations, that loop back on one another, demonstrating the surreal actions of alienated protagonists. (...) It is a crowded, teeming tone, but the reward is an off-kilter precision, one that feels both untainted and unique. Playing from memory (quoting gestures and attitudes), with reportage and documentary, the episodes narrate in a matter-of-factness that excludes all doubt and misunderstanding about the incidents in question. How do we know what is true in the world and in ourself? The Chorus' communal act of asking keeps the reader/spectator, for a time (off-duty), from the dark and cold.

Roberta Allegria (Santiago de Chile)

Bodin writes with uncommon narrative authority, conjuring the retrospective of a nurse for a dictator with extraordinary psychological precision. He incarnates voices, that embody history, its scale and force. In **The Nurse** the past is shadowy, rumbling from a distance, apprehended in ideologies and half-truths. One is confronted with an improbable blend of transgression and redemption, piety and defiance; comforting need and unsettling images; and, topping all of these, the choices people make when deciding which stories to tell or to depict. (...) Metaphors slide out of clipped fragments, torque themselves from sentences pell-mell and complex. (...) It's not always easy to care about these characters: detailed as they are, they remain types around whom description and metaphor are formed. Bodin creates plenty of intensity in small moments of lyric stasis.

Antonio Presto (Naples, Italy)

"I speak to those, who know" – writes Bodin in his **Half the Sky**. (...) His texts jump from ancient history to contemporary life, from reality to fantasy. It is worth reading them one after another, to get a full impression of the authors way of thinking and his point of view of our world. Every test is only a small aspect of his mosaic. Each element is representative of the whole. The material is a combination of different, sometimes opposite themes and styles. Bodin uses this discord for clear expression of his position to awake the readers reaction. This attitude shows how close Bodin's poetic is to Brecht's. In a sense Bodin continues Brecht's legacy into the present day.

Alla Sosnovskaya (Haifa, Israel)

Bodin's plays depict human life in time, reflecting the modern world. A rich variety of individual stories stand for a collective truth. The character's inner conflict collides with historical circumstances and this creates a dialectical unity of antagonistic tension. In this striking dramatic texts, Bodin is both clever and observant, and the effect is vastly affecting.

Paul Tseng (Taipeh, Republic of China)

A "theatre maker", who strips away the excesses of realistic dialogue, and writes with a compressed lyrical intensity, reminding the reader of Lorca, Ionesco, Beckett and a poet like Anne Carson. With his customary knack for scenes and characters chiseled with a stone cutter's economy, Bodin constructs in **Half the City** a world of dozens of glistering miniatures and tossed-off portraits, each bristling with life.

Charles Helmetag (Philadelphia, USA)